What Living Things Need

Food

Vic Parker

www.raintreepublishers.co.uk
Visit our website to find out more information about **Raintree** books.

To order:

 Phone 44 (0) 1865 888112

 Send a fax to 44 (0) 1865 314091

 Visit the Raintree Bookshop at **www.raintreepublishers.co.uk** to browse our catalogue and order online.

First published in Great Britain by Raintree, Halley Court, Jordan Hill, Oxford OX2 8EJ, part of Harcourt Education.
Raintree is a registered trademark of Harcourt Education Ltd.

Editorial: Jilly Attwood and Kathy Peltan
Design: Jo Hinton-Malivoire and Bigtop
Picture Research: Ruth Blair and Andrea Sadler
Production: Séverine Ribierre

Originated by Modern Age House Ltd, Hong Kong
Printed and bound in China by South China Printing Company

10 digit ISBN 1 406 20037 9
13 digit ISBN 978 1 406 20037 9

10 09 08 07 06
10 9 8 7 6 5 4 3 2 1

British Library Cataloguing in Publication Data
Parker, Victoria
Food. – (What living things need)
572.4
A full catalogue record for this book is available from the British Library.

Acknowledgements
The publishers would like to thank the following for permission to reproduce photographs: Alamy p. **5**; Corbis pp. **6** (Ariel Skelley), **12**, **14**, **19**, **23** (farm), back cover (orange); FLPA pp. **15** (E & D Hosking), **16** (B. Borrell Casals), **17** (Foto Natura Stock), **18** (Gerard Lacz), **23** (insects, B. Borrell Casals), **23** (bamboo, Gerard Lacz), back cover (ladybird, B. Borrell Casals); Getty Images pp. **7** (Taxi), **20** (Photodisc), **22** (child, Digital Vision), **22** (bone, Photodisc), **22** (dog, Photodisc), **22** (rabbit, Photodisc); Harcourt Education Ltd pp. **13**, **23** (market); Harcourt Education Ltd (cornflakes, Tudor Photography) p. **22**; KPT Power Photos p. **22** (carrot); NHPA (A.N.T. Photo Library) p. **21**; Photolibrary.com pp. **4**, **11**; Powerstock (Maureen Lawrence) pp. **8**, **23** (energy); TopFoto pp. **9** (Bob Daemmrich, The Image Works), **10** (Esbin-Anderson, The Image Works).

Cover photograph reproduced with permission of Corbis.

The publishers would like to thank Michael Scott for his assistance in the preparation of this book.

Every effort has been made to contact copyright holders of any material reproduced in this book. Any omissions will be rectified in subsequent printings if notice is given to the publishers.

The paper used to print this book comes from sustainable resources.

Contents

What is a living thing? 4

What is food? 6

Why do we need food? 8

What food do we need? 10

Where does our food come from? 12

How do animals get their food? 14

What do animals eat? 16

Do all animals eat other animals? 18

How do plants get food? 20

Can you guess? 22

Glossary 23

Index 24

Note to parents and teachers 24

Some words are shown in bold, **like this**. You can find them in the picture glossary on page 23.

What is a living thing?

Living things are things that grow.

People, animals, and plants are living things.

Which things in this picture are living and which are not?

What is food?

Food is everything that we
eat and drink.

Living things eat different types
of food.

Why do we need food?

We need food to live.

Food gives us **energy** to talk, think, and move.

Food helps us to grow.

If we do not eat food, we get hungry and feel ill.

What food do we need?

Every day we need to eat different types of food.

We need to eat fruit and vegetables because they are good for us.

If we eat too much food, we feel sick!

Where does our food come from?

Much of the food we eat comes from **farms**.

Some food is made into meals at factories.

We go to shops and **markets** to buy food.

How do animals get their food?

Some animals find their food.

This giraffe is looking for tasty leaves.

Some animals hunt for food.

This owl has just caught a mouse to eat.

What do animals eat?

Some animals eat other animals for food.

This ladybird eats **insects** like this greenfly.

Some animals eat plants as well as animals.

These fish eat plants and insects.

Do all animals eat other animals?

Some animals only eat plants.
They do not eat other animals.

This panda eats **bamboo** plants.

Horses only eat plants too.

They eat grass and hay.
Hay is dried grass.

How do plants get food?

Plants make their own food.

Plants mix sunlight, air, and water in their leaves to make food.

This plant makes its own food, but it also eats **insects**!

It is called a Venus flytrap.

Can you guess?

carrot

dog

bone

child

cereal

rabbit

Can you match these foods with the living things that eat them?

Glossary

 **bamboo** a leafy plant which has long, strong stems

 **energy** the ability to move and do things

 **farm** place where plants are grown and animals are raised for food

 **insects** animals with six legs, such as beetles

 **market** a place where people bring things to sell

Index

animals 4, 14, 15, 16, 17, 18

bamboo 18

factories 12

farms 12

fish 17

fruit 10

giraffe 14

grass 19

hay 19

horses 19

insects 16, 17, 21

ladybird 16

markets 13

meals 12

mouse 15

owl 15

panda 18

plants 4, 17, 18, 19, 20, 21

shops 13

vegetables 10

Note to parents and teachers

Reading non-fiction texts for information is an important part of a child's literacy development. Readers can be encouraged to ask simple questions and then use the text to find the answers. Most chapters in this book begin with a question. Read the questions together. Look at the pictures. Talk about what the answer might be. Then read the text to find out if your predictions were correct. To develop readers' enquiry skills, encourage them to think of other questions they might ask about the topic. Discuss where you could find the answers. Assist children in using the contents page, picture glossary and index to practise research skills and new vocabulary.

Titles in the *What Living Things Need* series include:

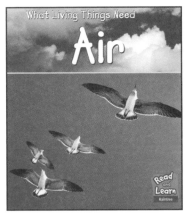

Hardback 1 406 20034 4

Hardback 1 406 20037 9

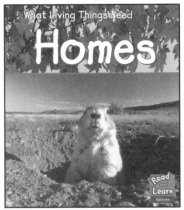

Hardback 1 406 20038 7

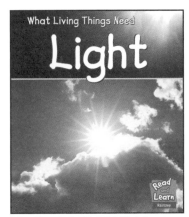

Hardback 1 406 20036 0

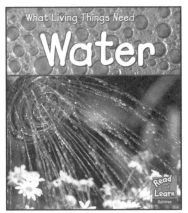

Hardback 1 406 20035 2

Find out about the other titles in this series on our website www.raintreepublishers.co.uk